Coming of Age

Coming of Age

Essential Literary Themes

by Valerie Bodden

Essential Library

An Imprint of Abdo Publishing | abdopublishing.com

abdopublishing.com

Published by Abdo Publishing, a division of ABDO, PO Box 398166, Minneapolis, Minnesota 55439. Copyright © 2016 by Abdo Consulting Group, Inc. International copyrights reserved in all countries. No part of this book may be reproduced in any form without written permission from the publisher. Essential Library™ is a trademark and logo of Abdo Publishing.

Printed in the United States of America, North Mankato, Minnesota
052015
092015

Cover Photo: Shutterstock Images
Interior Photos: Everett Collection, 13, 16, 19, 25; Paramount Pictures/Photofest, 21, 30; iStock/Thinkstock, 23, 39, 55; John Bramley/Summit Entertainment/Everett Collection, 35, 42; Advertising Archive/Everett Collection, 40; Summit Entertainment/Photofest, 45, 47, 52; Buena Vista Pictures/Everett Collection, 61, 64, 71; David Bloomer/Weinstein Company/Everett Collection, 69; Weinstein Company/Everett Collection, 74, 76; James Bridges/20th Century Fox Film Corps/Everett Collection, 83, 86, 89; Fox 2000 Pictures/Everett Collection, 91; James Bridges/Fox 2000 Pictures/Everett Collection, 95, 96

Editor: Angela Wiechmann
Series Designer: Maggie Villaume

Library of Congress Control Number: 2015931034
Cataloging-in-Publication Data

Bodden, Valerie.
 Coming of age / Valerie Bodden.
 p. cm. -- (Essential literary themes)
Includes bibliographical references and index.
ISBN 978-1-62403-803-7
1. American literature--Themes, motives--Juvenile literature. 2. American literature--History and criticism--Juvenile literature. I. Title.
810--dc23

                                        2015931034

Contents

1

INTRODUCTION TO
Themes in Literature

*D*o you find yourself drawn to the same types of stories? Are your favorite characters on a quest? Are they seeking revenge? Or are your favorite stories about love? Love, revenge, a quest—these are all examples of themes. Although each story is different, many stories focus on similar themes. You can expand your understanding of the books you read by recognizing the common themes within them.

What Is a Theme?

A theme is a concept or idea that shows up again and again in various works of art, literature, music, theater, film, and other endeavors throughout history. Some themes revolve around a story's plot. For example, a play about a young girl moving away from home and learning the ways of the world would be considered a coming of age story. But themes are not always so easily noticed. For example, a work might have allusions. Allusions are references, sometimes indirect, to other works or historical events. Themes might also relate to specific characters or subjects of a work. For example, many stories present heroes or villains. These common character types are often called archetypes.

How Do You Uncover a Theme?

Themes are presented in different ways in different works, so you may not always be aware of them. Many works have multiple themes. Uncover themes by asking yourself questions about the work. What is the main point or lesson of the story? What is the main conflict? What do the characters want? Where does the story take place? In many cases, themes may not be apparent until after a close study, or analysis, of the text.

What Is an Analysis?

Writing an analysis allows you to explore the themes in a work. In an analysis, you can consider themes in multiple ways. You can describe what themes are present in a work. You can compare one work to another to see how the presentation of a theme differs between the two forms. You can see how the use of a particular theme either supports or rejects society's norms. Rather than attempt to discover the author's purpose in creating a work, an analysis reveals what *you* see in the work.

Raising your awareness of themes through analysis allows you to dive deeper into the work itself. You may begin to see similarities between all creative works that you encounter. You may also improve your own writing by expanding your understanding of how stories use themes to engage readers.

Forming a Thesis

Form your questions about how a theme is presented in a work or multiple works and find answers within the work itself. Then you can create a thesis. The thesis is the key point in your analysis. It is your argument about the work. For example, if you want to argue that the theme of a book is love, your thesis could be worded as follows: Allison Becket's novel *On the Heartless Road* asserts that receiving love is critical to the human experience.

How to Make a Thesis Statement

In an analysis, a thesis statement typically appears at the end of the introductory paragraph. It is usually only one sentence long and states the author's main idea.

Providing Evidence

Once you have formed a thesis, you must provide evidence to support it. Evidence will usually take the form of examples and quotations from the work itself, often including dialogue from a character. You may wish to address what others have written about the work. Quotes from these individuals may help support your claim. If you find any quotes or examples that contradict your thesis, you will need to create an argument against them. For instance: Many critics claim the theme of love is secondary to that of revenge, as the main character, Carly, sabotages the lives of her loved ones throughout the novel. However, the novel's resolution proves that Carly's experience with love is the key to her humanity.

Concluding the Essay

After you have written several arguments and included evidence to support them, finish the essay with

How to Support a Thesis Statement

An analysis should include several arguments that support the thesis's claim. An argument is one or two sentences long and is supported by evidence from the work being discussed. Organize the arguments into paragraphs. These paragraphs make up the body of the analysis.

a conclusion. The conclusion restates the ideas from the thesis and summarizes some of the main points from the essay. The conclusion's final thought often considers additional implications for the essay or gives the reader something to ponder further.

How to Conclude an Essay

Begin your conclusion with a recap of the thesis and a brief summary of the most important or strongest arguments. Leave readers with a final thought that puts the essay in a larger context or considers its wider implications.

In This Book

In this book, you will read summaries of works, each followed by an analysis. Critical thinking sections will give you a chance to consider other theses and questions about the work. Did you agree with the author's analysis? What other questions are raised by the thesis and its arguments? You can also see other directions the author could have pursued to analyze the work. Then, in the Analyze It section in the final pages of this book, you will have an opportunity to create your own analysis paper.

The Theme of Coming of Age

The book you are reading focuses on the theme of coming of age. Also known as a bildungsroman (German for "novel of formation or education"), a coming of age story is one in which the protagonist, or main character, matures from childhood into adulthood. These stories often feature teenage protagonists dealing with the trials of growing up. Leaving childhood behind, the character may gain wisdom and a new sense of identity. But growing up also often means a loss of innocence as characters have to face the adult realities of the world. Race, gender, and socioeconomic standing can impact a character's coming of age, as can the historical time period and the society in which he or she lives.

Look for the Guides

Throughout the chapters that analyze the works, thesis statements have been highlighted. The box next to the thesis helps explain what questions are being raised about the work. Supporting arguments have also been highlighted. The boxes next to the arguments help explain how these points support the thesis. The conclusions are also accompanied by explanatory boxes. Look for these guides throughout each analysis.

2

AN OVERVIEW OF

A Separate Peace

*P*ublished in 1959, John Knowles's *A Separate Peace*
relates the coming of age of 16-year-old Gene Forrester,
a student at the Devon School, a boarding school in
New England during World War II (1939–1945).
Gene's journey into adulthood is set in motion by his
relationship with Finny, his best friend.

The novel opens with an adult Gene visiting the
school and reflecting on how it seems newer and yet
somehow museum-like. Gene slogs across muddy
playing fields in the rain to find a tree that looms large in
his memories. To his surprise, the tree is much smaller
and feebler than he remembered.

Gene climbs into the tree, about to make a terrifying leap.

The Summer Session

The narrative then switches to Gene's story as a 16-year-old during the 1942 Summer Session at Devon. Young Gene stands at the base of the tree with a group of boys and his best friend, Phineas, also called Finny. Finny climbs the tree to a high branch and then jumps into the river below. Afterward, Finny convinces Gene to jump too, even though Gene is secretly terrified.

Returning to jump from the tree again at Finny's insistence, Gene nearly loses his balance, and Finny steadies him. When later reflecting, Gene thinks Finny may have saved his life. But he also blames Finny for making him risk his life by jumping in the first place.

One summer day, Finny convinces Gene to break school rules and bike to the beach several hours away. While swimming, Gene is overtaken by a wave. Gene and Finny sleep on the beach and in the morning return to Devon just in time for Gene to take a trigonometry test. It is the first test he ever fails.

Boyhood Rivalry

That night as he catches up on his homework, Gene begins to suspect Finny is deliberately sabotaging his studies with constant distractions. He thinks Finny, a natural athlete but a poor student, wants to be better than him. These thoughts of rivalry drive Gene to work even harder at his studies.

At the end of Summer Session, Finny tries to pull Gene away from studying for his French exam to watch their friend Leper Lepellier—a known coward—jump from the tree. Gene is sure this is merely another attempt by Finny to sabotage his academics. He snaps at Finny. Surprised, Finny says he had assumed academics came naturally to Gene, just as athletics came naturally to Finny. Now he insists Gene stay behind to study. With bitterness, Gene realizes Finny had never been jealous. Gene admits Finny has always been the better person.

Finny's Fall

Gene goes to the tree with Finny, who insists they jump together. Finny makes his way out onto the branch. Gene follows, but he purposely jounces the tree limb. Finny looks at Gene with surprise, then he falls onto the bank below. Before he leaps from the limb into the river, Gene notes with some satisfaction how awkwardly Finny falls.

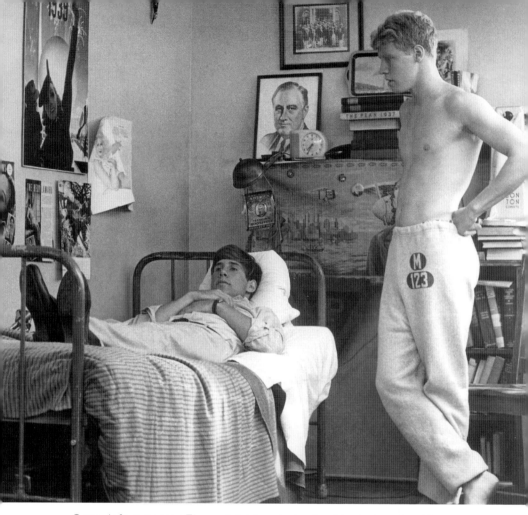

Gene, *left*, suspects Finny, *right*, is sabotaging him by keeping him from his studies.

Finny breaks his leg so badly he will never play sports again. After several days, Gene is allowed to visit Finny in the hospital. Gene is nervous and defensive as they discuss the fall. He expects Finny to blame him for the fall, but Finny does not seem to remember what happened. He says he has a feeling Gene was somehow involved, but he apologizes for even suggesting such a thing. Overwhelmed with guilt, Gene tries to tell

Finny the truth, but the doctor comes in, and Gene has to leave.

Winter Session

Summer Session ends with students returning to their homes. In September, Gene heads back to school for Winter Session, stopping at Finny's house in Boston, Massachusetts, on the way. Finny has not yet been cleared to return to school. Gene confesses to Finny that he caused the accident, but Finny angrily denies it. Gene realizes his confession hurts Finny even more than the accident did. He vows to take back the confession once they are in school.

By Thanksgiving, Finny has returned to school. He insists on training Gene for the 1944 Olympics. Even though Gene knows there will be no Olympics that year because of the war, the guilt of ending Finny's own athletic dreams spurs him to go along with the plan. He gets up early each morning to run. Eventually, Finny begins pulling Gene away from the other students.

Leper's Escape

As winter wears on, Finny convinces Gene and the other students to help him hold a Winter Carnival. For them, the day is an escape, but it comes to an end when Gene receives a telegram from Leper, who had enlisted in the army a few weeks before. The telegram says Leper has escaped from training camp and needs help.

Gene rides a train through the night to reach Leper's home in Vermont, where he learns Leper has suffered a nervous breakdown. Leper lashes out at Gene and accuses him of being "a savage underneath" and of knocking Finny out of the tree.[1] In response, Gene kicks over Leper's chair.

The Trial

One night soon afterward, class politician Brinker Hadley brings Gene and Finny to the Assembly Room in the First Building. There, Brinker and a group of his friends put Gene on mock trial for causing Finny's accident. Leper arrives, looking well and confident compared to his last visit with Gene. He says he saw both Gene and Finny in the tree at the time of the accident. He is hesitant to reveal more because he knows the truth is dangerous.

Crying, Finny says he does not care what happened. He lashes out at Brinker and rushes out of the room, leaning on the cane he still uses. Moments later,

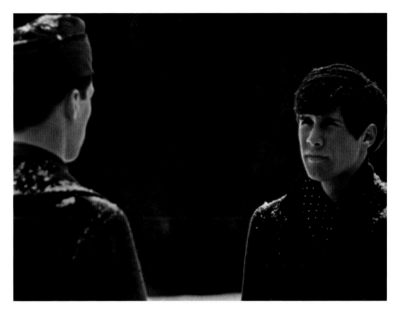

Gene goes to Vermont to help Leper, who has just deserted from the army.

the boys hear the sound of Finny crashing down the steps. The fall rebreaks his leg, and he is taken to the campus infirmary.

Confession and Forgiveness

The next day, Gene visits Finny in the infirmary and confesses again about what happened at the tree. Finny suggests Gene's actions that day in the tree had been a momentary impulse, rather than something personal. Gene agrees, though he admits he cannot understand how Finny could accept such an explanation. Finny says he believes Gene and forgives him.

Finny is scheduled for surgery to set the leg that afternoon. After attending classes, Gene returns to visit Finny. But the doctor reports that Finny died during surgery. Bone marrow entered his bloodstream, traveled to his heart, and stopped it. Gene attends Finny's funeral, but he does not cry for his friend. He states, "I could not escape a feeling that this was my own funeral, and you do not cry in that case."[2]

By June, the army has set up a Parachute Riggers' school on the Devon campus. Jeeps and troops overtake the school. The students discuss their enlistment plans. Gene says he will enlist in the navy to avoid being drafted into the infantry, the division that sees dangerous action on the front lines. He plans to enter training in a few weeks. He says he is ready for war because his hatred is gone, but he feels his war ended before he ever reached the battlefield.

As he heads to war, Gene reflects on the battles he has waged within himself.

3

The Symbolism of Coming of Age

A symbol is an object, person, or idea that stands for something else. Authors use symbols to give their writing layers of meaning. In most cases, a symbol retains its literal meaning but has a deeper, representational meaning as well. For example, an author might show a character drinking a glass of water. The character is literally drinking water, but on a deeper level, the water might be a symbol for life. Some symbols, especially colors, are universal. The color black usually symbolizes evil or death, for example. Other symbols are unique to specific books and must be interpreted based on the context in which they are used.

The tree is perhaps the most important symbol in
A Separate Peace.

Childhood is often considered a time of innocence. Therefore, the process of coming of age involves shedding that innocence and learning about the evil in the world—and in oneself. John Knowles's *A Separate Peace* chronicles Gene Forrester's journey through this process. Throughout the novel, Knowles uses symbolism to reflect Gene's coming of age as he moves from childhood innocence to adult acknowledgement of his own evil nature.

The novel opens during Summer Session at Devon School, with summer symbolizing childhood innocence. The summer mornings shine, reflecting the purity and innocence of a childhood untainted by evil. During the summer, only a few students

A carefree spirit, Finny represents summer.

attend school, and the teachers relax their rules. This symbolizes the carefree days of childhood. Finny too is a symbol of summertime innocence. He likes and charms everyone—teachers included—even though he rarely follows the rules. He even convinces rule-abiding Gene to take an overnight trip to the beach. But on that trip, Gene begins to feel out of control in this relaxed, summertime atmosphere. He gets caught in a wave that "rushed me from the control of gravity and took control of me itself; the wave threw me down in a primitive plunge without a bottom."[1] This plunge symbolizes the moral plunge Gene is about to take from childhood innocence to adulthood.

Argument Two

In the second argument, the author focuses on a specific symbol found during the Summer Session, the tree: "Gene's coming of age begins at the tree, which symbolizes his fear."

Gene's coming of age begins at the tree, which symbolizes his fear. "This tree flooded me with a sensation of alarm all the way to my tingling fingers," he says.[2] Specifically, the tree becomes a symbol of Gene's fears about his friendship with Finny, as Finny urges him to jump from it. Gene resents Finny shaming him into jumping, and this resentment builds into paranoia that Finny is sabotaging him. When Gene learns his suspicions are untrue, however, he is forced to acknowledge his own evil nature for the first time. Gene resents that Finny is actually a better person than he is. Now, Gene is afraid not of the tree but of himself: "Any fear I had ever had of the tree was nothing beside this. It wasn't my neck, but my understanding which was menaced."[3] Unwilling to face the worst in himself, Gene impulsively bounces the tree branch, causing his friend to lose his balance and slip. Finny's horrible fall symbolizes Gene's jealous desire to bring Finny down, to sabotage him. Seeing Finny injured on the bank below, Gene then jumps into the water with "every trace of my fear . . . forgotten."[4]

Afterward, the students enter the Winter Session, with winter symbolizing adulthood. As the masters return, they scatter "the easygoing summer spirit like so many fallen leaves."[5] While Finny, the symbol of summer, recovers at home, straightlaced Brinker Hadley takes over class leadership. Dressing like an adult in a dark, heavy suit, Brinker symbolizes the darkness of winter and the adult world. His clothing forms a stark contrast to Finny's pink shirt and use of a school tie for a belt. Finny, with his summertime attitude, returns to campus after the first snow. Gene feels the ice and snow—not to mention the slick marble floors—are dangerous for Finny, who must navigate them with his crutches. Gene worries Finny will be hurt by winter—or, symbolically, by adulthood. The only bright spot is when Finny organizes a Winter Carnival. The day, like summer, seems to offer a reprieve from the encroaching pressures of adulthood.

Argument Three

This paragraph presents the third argument: "Afterward, the students enter the Winter Session, with winter symbolizing adulthood." Paralleling the paragraph about the Summer Session, this paragraph will focus on how the Winter Session is a symbol of adulthood.

It provides a "momentary, illusory, special and separate peace."[6] But the peace cannot last. The carnival ends when Gene receives a plea from his friend Leper Lepellier, who has deserted from the army and the harsh realities of adulthood it represents.

The looming war is yet another symbol of the change from childhood to adulthood. In the summer, the war—a universal symbol of conflict—has only minor impact on the Devon campus. The jump from the tree starts as a war-training exercise for older students, for example. But by the end of the winter, war activities have increased and recruiting officers make frequent visits to the school. Even as his classmates make plans to enlist, Gene does nothing. He says, "I didn't feel free to [enlist], and I didn't know why this was so."[7] Symbolically, Gene is not ready to pass into the adulthood war symbolizes because he has not yet faced his guilt about his dark side.

Argument Four

The fourth argument focuses on another specific symbol, the war, which encroaches on the Winter Session: "The looming war is yet another symbol of the change from childhood to adulthood."

28

When Gene acknowledges his own evil nature at the end of the Winter Session, he is finally able to come of age. **When Brinker brings Gene and Finny to the First Building for Gene's mock trial, Gene notices the inscription above the door: "Here Boys Come to Be Made Men."[8] The inscription symbolizes the change in Gene that begins with the trial. After Finny flees from the trial and rebreaks his leg in another fall, Gene is finally able to confess to his friend. In this confession, Gene acknowledges his own evil nature, saying it was "some ignorance inside me, some crazy thing inside me, something blind, that's all it was."[9] This confession—and Finny's forgiveness—is Gene's first step to come of age. When Finny dies during surgery shortly after, Gene fully admits the blame falls on him: "Nothing as [Finny] was growing up at home, nothing at Devon, nothing even about the war had broken his harmonious and natural unity. So at last had I."[10] With this final acknowledgement, Gene is ready to enter the

Having come of age, Gene feels ready to join the war effort.

often harsh world of adulthood, enlisting in the war shortly afterward.

Gene's coming of age experience is sparked by seemingly innocent events at the tree at the end of the Summer Session. The rich symbolism in *A Separate Peace* presents many dimensions of his transition from childhood innocence to adulthood acknowledgement of evil. By the end of the novel, Gene has finally faced the evil in himself and can go into the war without hatred. He has already fought his worst enemy—himself—and won.

Conclusion

The final paragraph concludes the critique by summing up the arguments and partially restating the thesis, which has now been backed up with evidence.

Thinking Critically

Now it is your turn to assess the essay. Consider these questions:

1. The thesis emphasizes the role of symbols in representing Gene's coming of age. Do you think the story would be as effective without these symbols?

2. The author argues the Summer Session is a symbol of childhood innocence while the Winter Session is a symbol of adulthood. What else could the two sessions symbolize?

3. The critique concludes that Gene could not come of age until he recognized his own evil nature. Do you think he truly recognizes this? If so, do you think that recognition changed him?

Other Approaches

What you have just read is one possible way to analyze the symbolism in *A Separate Peace*. What are some other ways to approach symbolism in this novel? Remember that symbols stand for more than their surface meaning. The following are two alternate approaches.

Becoming Finny

At the beginning of *A Separate Peace*, Gene is insecure about his own identity, but after Finny's fall, Gene's identity seems to merge with that of his friend. Gene dresses in Finny's clothes and trains for the Olympics because Finny's own athletic dreams are over. And when Finny dies, Gene feels he is at his own funeral. The thesis statement for a critique based on the symbolism of Gene and Finny's shared identity might be: As he comes of age, Gene symbolically becomes Finny.

Sports as a Symbol

Sports play a large role in life on the Devon campus. In the beginning, the boys enjoy carefree games of Finny's invention. After Finny's fall robs him of his athletic gifts, he rigorously trains Gene for the Olympics. And in the end, the campus is overtaken with war-training exercises. How athletic activities change throughout the novel symbolizes the boys' coming of age. The thesis statement for a critique on the symbolism of sports in the novel might be: Gene's coming of age is reflected through the evolution of athletics on the Devon campus.

4

AN OVERVIEW OF

The Catcher in the Rye and *The Perks of Being a Wallflower*

J. D. Salinger's 1951 novel, *The Catcher in the Rye*, is considered a classic coming of age story. The novel relates the experiences of Holden Caulfield, a 17-year-old boy who must come to terms with the "phoniness" of the adult world he is about to enter.[1] As a modern coming of age tale, the 2012 film *The Perks of Being a Wallflower* is based on Stephen Chbosky's

Similar to Holden Caulfield, Charlie Kelmeckis is on the brink of adulthood.

1999 novel of the same name. The film follows Charlie Kelmeckis through his freshman year of high school.

The Catcher in the Rye

As the novel opens, the reader learns that last Christmas, Holden was treated for some sort of mental breakdown. He admits his life has been difficult. Throughout the novel, he relates the events leading to that breakdown.

Holden begins by describing what happens just after he is kicked out of Pencey Prep, a Pennsylvania boarding school. In a few days, he will have to return home. His roommate, Ward Stradlater, known as Stradlater, announces he has a date with Jane Gallagher. Holden is excited to hear her name. She was his neighbor two summers ago, and they spent a lot of time talking and playing checkers.

All night, Holden frets about Stradlater's date with Jane. When Stradlater returns, Holden tries to discover if he kissed Jane. Stradlater will not answer, so Holden throws a weak punch. Stradlater fights back and knocks Holden to the ground.

Escape to New York

After the fight, Holden decides to leave Pencey immediately. He cannot go home, though, because his parents do not know he has been kicked out of school. Instead, he takes the train to New York City, where he checks into a hotel. He has a prostitute sent to his room, but when she arrives, he feels awkward and depressed. He does not sleep with her after all. Afterward, the prostitute brings another man to confront Holden about the payment, and the man punches him.

The next day, Holden calls up Sally Hayes, a girl he used to date, even though he says she is a phony. They make plans to see a matinee play, and the date goes horribly, with Holden upsetting Sally.

Later that night, Holden meets up with Luce, an acquaintance from one of his old schools. Luce recommends Holden see a psychoanalyst for therapy. After drinking too much, Holden decides to walk to the park.

Being the Catcher in the Rye

It is cold outside in the park. Holden worries he will catch pneumonia, so he decides to sneak into his house, which is nearby. He wants to see his little sister, Phoebe.

Seeing Phoebe makes him feel better, but she deduces he was kicked out of school. She says, "Daddy'll kill you!"[2]

As they talk, Holden confides in her he wants to be the "catcher in the rye," misquoting a line from Scottish poet Robert Burns: "If a body meet a body coming through the rye."[3] Holden imagines his job will be to watch over children playing in a big field of rye, catching them if they get too close to the cliff.

The next day, Holden visits Mr. and Mrs. Antolini, family friends. Mr. Antolini expresses concern about Holden's future and well-being. Holden stays the night, only to wake suddenly to Mr. Antolini sitting next to him, patting his head. Very uncomfortable, Holden leaves at once. He says, "That kind of stuff's happened to me about twenty times since I was a kid."[4]

As he is walking down the street, Holden has delusions that he is disappearing. He asks his younger brother, Allie—who died of leukemia when Holden was only 13—not to let him disappear. He makes a plan to run away, hitchhiking west to assume a new identity as a deaf-mute. But first he wants to say good-bye to Phoebe, so he leaves her instructions to meet him at the museum. Phoebe arrives at the museum with a suitcase and begs Holden to take her with him. Imagining Phoebe leaving

Losing grip on reality, Holden worries he is disappearing.

home makes Holden change his own mind about leaving. He takes her to the zoo and lets her ride on the carousel as he watches.

The story concludes with Holden in the hospital recovering from a breakdown. He admits he is not sure how he feels about the events leading to his breakdown. He is not quite sure how life will go at a new school

The Catcher in the Rye

J. D. SALINGER

Holden lets Phoebe, his younger sister, enjoy a carousel ride.

either. He thinks he will apply himself this time, but he cannot be sure.

The Perks of Being a Wallflower

The movie opens with Charlie writing a letter to someone he addresses simply as "friend."[5] He writes that he recently spent time in the hospital. Tomorrow is his first day as a high school freshman, and he needs to turn things around. But the first day of school does not go well, as he sits alone at lunch and does not make any friends. The pattern repeats for several days.

Befriended

One evening Charlie goes to a football game, where he is befriended by Patrick, a senior from his shop class. Charlie remembers how their shop teacher had insulted Patrick in front of the whole class. Patrick introduces Charlie to his stepsister, Sam, who is also a senior. Arriving back home, Charlie sees his sister, Candace, getting hit in the face by her boyfriend. She begs him not to tell their parents as she continues to see her boyfriend.

Charlie joins Sam, Patrick, and their circle of friends at the homecoming dance. He goes to a party afterward, where he eats a brownie laced with marijuana. That night, he tells Sam his best friend, Michael, shot himself the year before. While Sam reels from the news, Charlie

Sam throws her arms into the air as they speed through a tunnel.

looks for the bathroom and accidentally walks in on Patrick kissing Brad, a football player. Charlie promises to keep their relationship a secret.

After the party, Sam and Patrick drive Charlie through a tunnel as they blast the radio. Sam climbs through the window into the pickup bed, where she stands with her arms outstretched as they emerge from the tunnel into a view of the city lights. Over the next weeks, Charlie spends most of his time with his new friends.

On Christmas Eve, which is also his birthday, Charlie has flashbacks of his aunt Helen, who was killed in a car accident on Christmas Eve when he was a little boy. She had been going to get his birthday present.

A Total Disaster

Sam's friend Mary Elizabeth invites Charlie to the Sadie Hawkins dance. Afterward, she calls Charlie her boyfriend. Charlie does not really want to go out with her, but he does not want to hurt her feelings either, so he goes along with it. He soon feels smothered by the relationship.

One night, Charlie and his friends are playing Truth or Dare, and Charlie is dared to kiss the prettiest girl in the room. To everyone's surprise, he kisses Sam. Both she and Mary Elizabeth storm out. Charlie wants to follow them to apologize, but Patrick says he should stay away to let the tension die down in their circle of friends.

Charlie goes two weeks without seeing his friends. The flashbacks of Aunt Helen become more frequent, including memories of her confiding in him about her own traumatic, abusive past. Charlie writes to his friend that he's "starting to get bad again."[6]

Friends Again

Charlie learns Patrick and Brad have broken up. He feels terrible when Brad insults Patrick in front of everyone in the cafeteria. Three of Brad's football teammates attack Patrick, and Charlie jumps in to help his friend. The next thing he knows, all three of the football players are on the ground, and Charlie's hand is bruised and swollen. He has single-handedly beaten up all of them, though he cannot fully remember it.

After the fight, Charlie's friends accept him into their circle again. On the last day of school, Charlie helps them celebrate their graduation.

Remembering

After Sam's graduation party, she and Charlie go up to her room for some time alone. They confess their feelings for one another and start to kiss. As the kiss builds, Sam rubs Charlie's leg. He suddenly pulls away, looking shocked and scared. Sam asks him what is wrong, but he says it is nothing.

The next day, Sam leaves for the summer session at college. Charlie kisses her good-bye and then walks home, having flashbacks along the way. He remembers Aunt Helen sexually abusing him and rubbing his leg the way Sam did. Aunt Helen had told him it was a secret between them. When he gets home, the flashbacks continue, and he cannot stop crying. No one else is there.

Being with Sam stirs memories Charlie has long forgotten.

Finally, he calls his sister, who is at a friend's house. He tells her he must have killed Aunt Helen—and maybe he even wanted her to die. His sister has a friend send the police to her house as Charlie hangs up. Distraught, he goes into the kitchen and sees a knife on the counter. Right at that moment, the police break down the door.

Charlie wakes up in a psychiatric hospital, where he eventually tells the doctor that Aunt Helen abused him. Charlie returns home at the end of summer, and Patrick and Sam visit. They go for a drive through the tunnel. This time, it is Charlie who climbs into the back of the truck and stands with his arms outstretched as they emerge into the city lights.

Psychology and Coming of Age

*P*sychology involves the study of the mind and behavior. It examines not only what people do but also why they do it—their motivations. Psychological criticism interprets a literary work in light of specific psychological theories, such as those advanced by leading psychologists Sigmund Freud, B. F. Skinner, or Abraham Maslow. A critic can even use his or her own psychological theories to analyze a work.

In some cases, psychological criticism involves examining an author's unconscious motivations in writing a work. In other cases, it analyzes the psychology of literary characters, viewing them as if

Both Charlie and Holden face psychological obstacles as they come of age.

they were real people with unconscious desires. Other methods examine how the reader's own psychology might influence his or her interpretation of a work.

From a psychological perspective, the experience of coming of age can be full of difficulties, the roots of which may lie deep in the unconscious. Both *The Catcher in the Rye* and *The Perks of Being a Wallflower* present characters who rely on defense mechanisms to protect themselves from traumatic childhood experiences and the difficulty of growing up. In psychology, a defense mechanism is an unconscious process in which a person conceals certain memories or feelings from the conscious mind. After suffering mental breakdowns, Holden and Charlie are forced to face their psychological pain without defense mechanisms, which allows them to finally come of age.

Both Holden from *The Catcher in the Rye* and Charlie from *The Perks of Being a Wallflower* suffered traumatic childhood experiences. Holden opens his story by saying he does not want to talk about his "lousy childhood."[1] When Holden was only 13, his younger brother, Allie, died of leukemia. Holden was so upset he slept in the garage and punched out all the windows with his bare fist. Later, when Holden attended one of many high schools, a classmate committed suicide while wearing Holden's sweater.

Argument One

This is the first argument: "Both Holden from *The Catcher in the Rye* and Charlie from *The Perks of Being a Wallflower* suffered traumatic childhood experiences." This idea will be supported by examples of Holden's and Charlie's traumatic experiences.

Charlie has dealt with his share of childhood trauma as well. When he was a young boy, his aunt Helen was killed in a car accident while shopping for his birthday present. Her death plagues him. A year before the events in the story, Charlie's best friend committed suicide. Charlie writes that he spent some time in the hospital before high school begins. And when Sam kisses him and passionately rubs his leg, Charlie suddenly remembers another traumatic event, yet again involving Aunt Helen:

Argument Two

The second argument relates to Holden's and Charlie's emotional natures: "Perhaps because of their trauma, Holden and Charlie are uniquely sensitive to emotional pain—both their own and others'."

she molested him. He begins questioning whether he wanted her to die.

Perhaps because of their trauma, Holden and Charlie are uniquely sensitive to emotional pain—both their own and others'. Holden often complains of being lonesome and depressed, saying, "I almost wished I was dead."[2] He breaks down in tears on several occasions, including when Stradlater punches him and when he leaves Pencey. In addition, others' pain upsets Holden. Holden is upset when students make fun of Robert Ackley, even though Holden himself is not fond of the student. Later, he fixates on a time when Jane was crying. "I don't know why, but it bothered the hell out of me," he says.[3] Even Holden's wish to be the "catcher in the rye" reflects his desire to protect innocent children from pain and harm.[4] It is a sentiment no doubt stemming from his brother Allie's death.

Like Holden, Charlie is sensitive to pain. Perhaps even more than Holden, however, Charlie is affected by other people's pain, which he wants to take from them.

He has constant flashbacks of holding Aunt Helen's hand as she cried about her abusive past. He also wants to rescue his sister from her abusive boyfriend, though she refuses help. After kissing Sam during Truth or Dare, he feels horrible for causing turmoil in their circle of friends. Charlie also feels terrible when the shop teacher says Patrick is "nothing."[5] So when Brad's friends attack Patrick, Charlie jumps to his defense, even though he is not fully aware of his own actions.

In order to separate from the pain, both Holden and Charlie rely on defense mechanisms. One of the defense mechanisms Holden employs is regression. Although he is 17, Holden says, "Some times I act like I'm about thirteen," and he holds a close connection with his younger sister, Phoebe.[6] Another mechanism Holden relies on is rationalization, where an acceptable explanation for one's behavior is substituted for the truth. Regarding his school expulsions, Holden makes excuses such as "they give guys the ax quite frequently at

Argument Three

This is the third argument: "In order to separate from the pain, both Holden and Charlie rely on defense mechanisms." The author will follow this with evidence showing how the characters use defense mechanisms.

When Patrick is insulted and attacked, Charlie rushes to defend him.

Pencey."[7] Such rationalizations keep him from admitting his expulsions stem from the fact he is avoiding graduation and the adult world. Holden's relationships with women are examples of displacement. Holden has feelings for Jane but has never acted on them. Instead, he jealously punches Stradlater after his date with Jane, invites a prostitute to his hotel room, and goes out with a girl he considers a phony. These actions displace his true, grown-up feelings for Jane.

Charlie uses his own set of defense mechanisms to deal with painful experiences. Repression involves burying certain thoughts or memories deep in the unconscious mind. Having repressed the memories of his molestation for years, Charlie suddenly remembers them when Sam rubs his leg. In addition, he uses the defense mechanism of reaction formation. Aunt Helen abused Charlie, but instead of admitting this to himself, he views her as his "favorite person in the world."[8] Other times, he demonstrates intellectualization, where he overanalyzes his feelings to avoid acting on them. He often fantasizes about Sam but never acts on his desires. He intellectualizes that he did not think she wanted him to ask her out.

Ultimately, Holden's and Charlie's defense mechanisms are unable to protect them, and both characters suffer mental breakdowns. As soon as he leaves Pencey, Holden feels as if his "nerves were shot."[9] Within days, his mental state deteriorates to the point where he worries he will disappear whenever he crosses the street, and he begs his dead brother for help. Seemingly having lost touch with reality, Holden plans

Argument Four

The fourth argument focuses on what happens when the characters' defense mechanisms fail: "Ultimately, Holden's and Charlie's defense mechanisms are unable to protect them, and both characters suffer mental breakdowns."

to hitchhike west and start a new life as a deaf-mute so he will not have to talk to anyone ever again.

Charlie's breakdown occurs more gradually, though it is likely not the first time it has happened. He admits in his letter he has recently spent time in the hospital. On Christmas Eve, he suffers from flashbacks of Aunt Helen's death. Throughout the spring, his mental stability progressively worsens, especially after he kisses Sam during Truth or Dare and must stay away from his friends. Recognizing it as a breakdown, he fears he is "starting to get bad again."[10] After the fight in the cafeteria, he says he "can't turn it off this time."[11] The breakdown culminates after he says good-bye to Sam. He is bombarded by memories of the molestation and the events of the school year.

Argument Five

This is the final argument: "Their mental breakdowns force Holden and Charlie to deal with their psychological pain—and take their first steps toward coming of age." This argument will illustrate how dealing with their pain leads the characters to come of age.

Their mental breakdowns force Holden and Charlie to deal with their psychological pain—and take their first steps toward coming of age. Holden watches Phoebe grab for a ring on the carousel, worried she might fall, but says, "The thing with kids

As reality slips, Holden plans to run away and assume a new identity as a deaf-mute.

is, if they want to grab for the gold ring, you have to let them do it."[12] Underneath this sentiment about other children is the growing realization that he could not have protected himself from the pain he suffered as a child. It marks the beginning of his coming of age experience. As the book closes, Holden wonders if he is ready to apply himself at school—and thus grow up. He also admits he does not know what to think of his breakdown. This honesty is perhaps a sign of being ready to leave defense mechanisms aside as he faces adulthood.

Conclusion

The final paragraph is the conclusion. It summarizes the arguments and revisits the thesis.

Similar to Holden, Charlie is unsure about his recovery, but he feels he can "start putting these pieces together."[13] For Charlie, the first step of coming of age is admitting what Aunt Helen did. He tells the "friend" he might not have time to write any more letters "because I might be too busy trying to participate."[14] He will no longer let his defense mechanisms and fear of pain hold him back from life.

Although their mental breakdowns are painful experiences for Holden and Charlie, both characters come out of them with a new awareness. They have been forced to grow up, and they no longer need to rely on so many defense mechanisms to face their pasts or their futures. Neither character expects the adult world to be perfect or pain-free—but both are ready to face whatever it may bring.

Thinking Critically

Now it is your turn to assess the essay. Consider these questions:

1. The author contends that Holden and Charlie are uniquely sensitive to pain. Do you agree? Could they have dealt with that pain without employing defense mechanisms?

2. The thesis argues the characters' mental breakdowns enable them to come of age. Do you agree the characters have come of age? Could they have come of age without those breakdowns?

3. Based on this analysis, what message do you think these works send about the teenage years and human psychology?

Other Approaches

What you have just read is one possible way to apply psychological criticism to *The Catcher in the Rye* and *The Perks of Being a Wallflower*. What are some other ways of applying this approach? Remember, psychology has to do with a person's motivations, which are often unconscious. The following are two alternate approaches.

The Id, Ego, and Superego

Much of Freud's work centers on the idea that the mind is divided into three parts: the id, the ego, and the superego. The id controls primitive instincts, such as hunger, while the superego reflects the rules an individual has learned from society. The ego attempts to strike a balance between the desires of the id and the superego. A thesis analyzing the role of the id, ego, and superego in these works might be: As they come of age, Holden and Charlie must address their warring ids, egos, and superegos in order to learn who they really are and how they fit into society.

Holden, Charlie, and Adlerian Psychology

In the 1800s, Austrian psychiatrist Alfred Adler proposed a system of psychology that emphasizes the goals and motivations behind human behavior. His system states that feelings of inferiority could lead either to great achievements or to psychological problems. A thesis analyzing these works from an Adlerian viewpoint might be: Holden and Charlie must face their feelings of inferiority before they are ready to come of age and move into adulthood.

AN OVERVIEW OF

The Adventures of Huckleberry Finn and *The Giver*

*P*ublished in 1884, Mark Twain's *The Adventures of Huckleberry Finn* follows 13-year-old Huckleberry Finn as he travels down the Mississippi River with Jim, a runaway slave. The novel has remained a classic for more than 100 years, although it often stirs up controversy for its use of a derogatory word to refer to African Americans. Twain used such language as part of his

Huckleberry Finn is a classic coming of age story.

realistic portrayal of Southern attitudes and language in the pre–Civil War South. Lois Lowry's 1993 novel, *The Giver,* takes place in a supposedly utopian society called the community, in which there is no conflict, war, starvation, or poverty. The community is strictly governed by rules that ensure equality and Sameness.

Huckleberry Finn

Huck begins his story by introducing himself to the reader, saying they might know him from Twain's novel *The Adventures of Tom Sawyer.* The Widow Douglas takes Huck into her home and tries to "sivilize" him, but he does not much like it.[1] He spends most of his time playing hooky with Tom, who enjoys adventures.

One day, Huck's father, a drunk he calls "pap," returns to town and snatches him from the widow's house. Pap is upset about money Huck found in his adventures with Tom. He keeps Huck locked in a cabin in the woods for two months, but Huck eventually manages to escape. He takes a canoe across the river and hides out on Jackson's Island. After a few days, he discovers Jim, an escaped slave he and Tom know from town. The two set out down the river on a raft, enjoying both adventures and lazy days along the way.

Soon they approach the Ohio River, which offers passage north to the Free States, where Jim will be safe. Huck now feels guilty for helping Jim escape from his owner, Miss Watson. He decides he must turn Jim in, but when he has the opportunity, he cannot bring himself to do it. After a while, Jim and Huck realize they have passed the mouth of the Ohio, so they have to continue downstream until they can find a canoe to paddle back upstream.

Back into Slavery

Huck and Jim come across two scam artists who refer to themselves as the king and the duke. Before Huck and Jim can rid themselves of the pair, the duke sells Jim to the Phelps family, claiming Jim is a runaway slave from near New Orleans, Louisiana. Huck debates whether he should notify Miss Watson but decides he would rather go to hell for helping a slave than turn Jim in. He plans to help Jim escape again, this time from the Phelpses.

Huck discovers Mr. and Mrs. Phelps are actually Tom Sawyer's Aunt Sally and Uncle Silas. When he shows up at their house, they assume he is Tom, and he plays along. When the real Tom Sawyer arrives a few days later, he agrees to take part in Huck's efforts

Huck is unsure whether he should turn in Jim or help him escape.

to free Jim. He convinces his aunt and uncle he is his brother, Sid.

The Escape

Huck comes up with a simple plan to rescue Jim immediately, but Tom objects. Instead, he sets up an elaborate plan to make things more difficult and adventurous. To add to the excitement, Tom leaves an anonymous letter to warn the Phelpses of the impending escape.

Tipped off by the letter, local farmers with guns converge on Jim's cabin. Huck, Tom, and Jim manage to escape as the farmers chase them, but Tom is shot in the leg. Once they are safe in their hiding place, Huck sends for the doctor. When the doctor arrives and discovers Jim, he ties up Jim and takes him back to Uncle Silas and Aunt Sally.

Tom is forced to reveal the news that Jim is not actually a slave—Miss Watson died two months earlier and set him free in her will. Tom had known it all along but never told Huck and Jim. When Aunt Sally asks Tom why they went to such lengths to "free" an already free slave, he says he "wanted the *adventure* of it."[2] When Tom's Aunt Polly arrives, she recognizes Tom and Huck and discloses their true identities.

As the book closes, Jim is free, and Tom plots an adventure for the three of them in Indian Territory, which is modern-day Oklahoma. Huck learns his pap is dead and Aunt Sally wants to adopt him. He decides he had better leave for Indian Territory instead, saying "she's going to . . . sivilize me, and I can't stand it. I been there before."[3]

The Giver

As *The Giver* opens, the protagonist, Jonas, is worried about the upcoming Ceremony of Twelve, in which he and all the other 12-year-olds will receive their work assignments. It is a special milestone. As another

milestone, Jonas begins taking pills to prevent the
Stirrings, or sexual desires, he begins experiencing in
his dreams.

A day before the ceremony, Jonas's father brings
home a newchild, a baby, who fusses at night and has not
been growing well. Jonas's father has been given special
permission to let the baby, Gabriel, sleep at the family's
home, as long as everyone in the family promises not to
get attached to him.

At the Ceremony of Twelve, Jonas nervously looks
forward to his assignment. But when his turn comes, the
Chief Elder skips over Jonas, who waits in agony. When
the other assignments have been handed out, the Chief
Elder calls Jonas forward and says he has been selected
as the next Receiver of Memory, the community's most
important Elder. Jonas is grateful yet afraid of what his
future holds.

Becoming Different

The next day, Jonas begins his training. Since Jonas is
the new Receiver, he is to call the old Receiver the
Giver. The Giver must transfer to Jonas all the memories
of the past he carries within him: "before you, before
me, before the previous Receiver, and generations before

him."[4] The Giver transmits these memories by touching Jonas's back. It will now be Jonas's job to keep these memories so the people of the community do not have to be burdened by them.

The first memory the Giver shares with Jonas is one of sledding. Then he gives him a memory of sunshine and warmth. He explains that snow, sunshine, and hills were all eliminated when the community adopted Sameness.

The Experience of Pain

As the weeks and months go by, the Giver begins to transmit memories of pain. In one memory, Jonas feels the pain of breaking a leg in a sledding accident. In others, he is neglected and underfed. Sometimes he receives memories of destruction and warfare, and in one he watches a young soldier die on the battlefield.

The Giver gives Jonas good memories as well, including his favorite: a family Christmas. Jonas cannot quite name the feeling the memory evokes, so the Giver tells him it is love. At home, Jonas begins bonding with Gabriel, transferring happy memories to him in the same way.

The Plan

As part of his assigned duties, Jonas's father must release a newchild. Jonas has heard about release many times but does not fully understand it. He believes it means the baby will be sent Elsewhere, somewhere outside the community, never to return. Aware of the truth, the Giver shows Jonas a video of the release. Jonas watches as his father matter-of-factly injects a syringe into the baby's forehead. When Jonas realizes "release" means killing, he weeps. He is horrified by the cold, cruel truth about the community.

Jonas refuses to go home that night. The Giver tells Jonas he must use his new emotions to help the community "change and become whole."[5] They make a plan: Jonas will secretly leave the community to go to the mysterious Elsewhere. When he leaves, his memories will be released back to the people. The Giver will stay to help the people learn to live with love, pain, and all the emotions of which they have been deprived.

The Escape

Jonas and the Giver decide to put their plan into action in two weeks. But when Jonas learns Gabriel is to be released the next day, he grabs the baby and makes his

Jonas and the Giver look over their plans for Jonas's escape to Elsewhere.

escape that night. He does not have time even to say good-bye to the Giver.

For many nights, Jonas bikes away from the community, carrying Gabriel with him. The two sleep during the day, hiding from the search planes flying overhead. After many days in the bitter cold, they run out of food, and Jonas fears they will starve.

As it begins to snow, Jonas comes to a hill and finds a sled. He and Gabriel slide down the hill "that seemed to lead to the final destination, the place that he had always felt was waiting, the Elsewhere that held their future and their past."[6] He sees a home ahead, decorated for Christmas, and he feels love and joy.

A Moralist View of Coming of Age

The word *moral* refers to whether an action is right or wrong. Moralist criticism analyzes the moral values in a work of art and how it depicts the right or wrong way of living. Moralist criticism might examine a character's actions in light of the morals of his or her society. Or it can analyze how the work represents the morality of an entire society's belief system.

The Adventures of Huckleberry Finn and *The Giver* present two very different worlds. The pre–Civil War South of *Huckleberry Finn* is marked by class and race distinctions. In contrast, the futuristic community of *The Giver* adheres to the principle of Sameness, in which class and

As he comes of age, Huck—like Jonas—questions his society's moral code.

Thesis

Argument One

race distinctions have been erased. Yet each of these societies lives by a clear moral code—which their protagonists come to see as corrupt. Huck and Jonas both come of age when they reject the immoral values of their societies.

Initially, both Huck and Jonas accept the morals of their societies. In the pre–Civil War South, slaves were not valued as human beings. When Huck and Tom come upon Jim sleeping under a tree, Tom suggests they should tie him up as a prank. Huck rejects the idea only for selfish reasons, not out of any concern for Jim. Later, as Jim and Huck make their way down the Mississippi, Huck's conscience troubles him for not returning Jim to Miss Watson. Like other Southerners of his day, Huck sees Jim as a piece of property. According to his society's moral code, it is wrong to keep such property from its owner. When Jim tells Huck he plans to rescue his family from slavery, Huck is angered that Jim "would steal his children—children that belonged to a man I didn't even know; a man that hadn't ever done me no harm."[1]

Like Huck, Jonas accepts his community's moral code. But unlike Huck, Jonas lives in a society where everyone is viewed equally. Despite his apprehension, Jonas is confident his community knows what is best for his future and that his Assignment will be right for him. As the Receiver, Jonas learns of a world filled with love and emotion, but he dismisses it in favor of the moral code he knows best. He believes an emotional society "wouldn't work very well. And that it's much better to be organized the way we are now. I can see that it was a *dangerous* way to live."[2]

Over time, both Huck and Jonas have conflicting emotions as they begin questioning their societies' values. As they travel, Huck begins to see Jim as a person.

Argument Two

The second argument focuses on how Huck and Jonas begin to doubt the morals they have been taught: "Over time, both Huck and Jonas have conflicting emotions as they begin questioning their societies' values."

When the Giver begins sharing memories filled with emotion, Jonas still favors the morals his society upholds.

When Huck agonizes about whether to turn in Jim, he is quite conflicted by what is right and wrong. He says, "I knowed very well I had done wrong" by not turning him in.[3] But then he considers how he would feel if he had "done right and give Jim up."[4] Huck also struggles as he reconsiders Jim's wish to free his family: "he cared just as much for his people as white folks does for their'n. It don't seem natural, but I reckon it's so."[5] Huck tries to reconcile what society believes, that slaves are property without feelings, with what he himself understands, that Jim is a human being who cares for his family.

Jonas's conflict with his society's moral code grows as he receives more and more memories. He recognizes what people have given up to have a painless life, and he is not sure the sacrifice is worthwhile. He desperately wants to share his new experiences with his friends, but they are content with their dull, emotionless lives. He stops taking the pills that prevent Stirrings because "he knew he couldn't go back to the world of no feelings that he had lived in so long."[6] Jonas's biggest moral conflict occurs as he watches a video of his father releasing a newchild. He feels "a ripping sensation inside himself, the feeling of terrible pain clawing its way forward to emerge in a cry."[7] He suddenly understands he and the Giver are the only ones in the community capable of seeing the killing of this child as wrong, because they are the only ones capable of feeling pain.

Huck and Jonas come of age when they follow their own consciences. For Huck, the defining moment comes when he tears up the letter he wrote Miss Watson about where Jim is. When he first writes the letter, he feels "all washed clean of sin," but then he starts thinking about Jim.[8] He studies the letter, "sort of holding my breath, and then says to myself: 'All right, then, I'll *go* to hell.'"[9] He tears it up. Huck knows he is sinning against society's morals and thinks he will go to hell for it. But he accepts his fate in order to save Jim. He makes his

Jonas is horrified once he learns what it means to release a baby.

first adult decision—one completely independent of the moral code surrounding him.

Jonas too comes of age by making an adult decision independent of his society's moral code. He rejects the community's insistence that love is meaningless; instead, he decides it is the only truly meaningful part of life. When first devising the escape plan, Jonas tries to convince the Giver to come with him, saying, "You and I don't need to *care* about the rest of them," but then he realizes, "Of course they needed to care. It was the meaning of everything."[10] When Jonas learns Gabriel is to be released, he must escape prematurely, fleeing with the baby during the night. His love for Gabriel spurs him to action despite the risk. When it is cold, he transmits memories of warmth because he feels "an urge, a need, a passionate yearning to share the warmth with the one person left for him to love."[11] As he leaves the community behind, he leaves behind its emotionless beliefs about love.

Huck's and Jonas's coming of age experiences show readers the inherent immorality in their societies' moral systems. Throughout *The Adventures of Huckleberry Finn*, Twain often uses irony to uphold Huck's morality versus Southern society's immorality. When Tom agrees to help him free Jim, Huck ironically says Tom "fell, considerable, in my estimation."[12] Although Huck himself wants to help Jim, he cannot believe Tom—the personification of the Southern moral code—would participate in such a "dirty, low-down business."[13] At the end, Huck completely severs ties with society rather than let it civilize him into following the moral code of rampant racism. The irony is a sharp criticism

Argument Four

The final argument explains the moral systems of Huck's and Jonas's societies are flawed: "Huck's and Jonas's coming of age experiences show readers the inherent immorality in their societies' moral systems."

of Southern immorality, highlighting Huck as the true moral authority.

As Jonas comes of age, he exposes the immorality in his own community's moral code. One of the most revealing and disturbing scenes in the novel occurs as Jonas watches his father release a newchild without even a trace of sadness. Shattered, Jonas understands the cost of living an emotionless life: it leads people to unwittingly commit immoral actions. Instead, Jonas upholds true morality, which can come only from feeling deeply and selflessly. When Gabriel is to be released according to the community's moral code, Jonas nearly sacrifices his own life to save him.

The worlds Huck and Jonas inhabit represent two extremes: one of unrelenting racism and one of complete equality. And yet both characters come to realize their societies are built upon flawed morals. In rejecting those morals, the characters are able to come of age and also illustrate to readers the danger of accepting such moral codes without question.

Conclusion

The final paragraph concludes the author's critique and sums up the arguments that support the thesis.

Thinking Critically

Now it is your turn to assess the essay. Consider these questions:

1. What additional arguments could the author have made about Huck's and Jonas's coming of age that would support the thesis?

2. The author argues Huck and Jonas turn away from their societies' moral codes. Do you think the author provides enough evidence of this?

3. The author's conclusion claims Huck and Jonas reveal the immorality of their societies. Do you agree? Why or why not?

Other Approaches

What you have just read is one possible way to apply moralist criticism to *The Adventures of Huckleberry Finn* and *The Giver*. Morality has to do with definitions of right and wrong. What are some other ways of applying this approach? Consider the following alternate approaches.

Taking the Easy Way Out

Neither Huck nor Jonas tries to reform his society. Instead, both ultimately flee—Huck out west, and Jonas to Elsewhere. A thesis based on this idea might be: Although both Huck and Jonas recognize the immorality of their societies, neither makes the adult decision to stay and fight for reforms.

Tackling Difficult Issues

The Adventures of Huckleberry Finn and *The Giver* tackle difficult subjects such as racism, abuse, euthanasia, and genetic engineering. Because of this, both books have at times been banned from schools and libraries. But some might argue that dealing with difficult issues is an essential part of coming of age—not only for the characters in a novel but also for readers. A thesis reflecting this concept might be: Reading about the difficult moral issues Huck and Jonas face as they come of age can help readers on their own coming of age journeys.

8

AN OVERVIEW OF
The Fault in Our Stars

John Green's 2012 novel, *The Fault in Our Stars,* recounts the story of Hazel Grace Lancaster, a 16-year-old girl with terminal cancer—"thyroid originally but with an impressive and long-settled satellite colony in my lungs."[1] A cancer drug has extended her life, though no one knows for how long. She needs an oxygen tank to deliver air to her nose through a tube.

The New Boy

At a support group meeting for teens with cancer, Hazel meets Augustus Waters, also known as Gus, a handsome 17-year-old who has lost his leg to osteosarcoma, a form

Teenagers Hazel and Gus both battle cancer in *The Fault in Our Stars*.

of bone cancer. With his cancer in remission, he is in better health than Hazel. After the meeting, Gus flirts with Hazel and invites her to his house. Hazel is amazed someone like him is interested in her. But then he pulls out a pack of cigarettes, and she thinks he has ruined everything. Gus explains he does not actually light the cigarettes. He sees them as a metaphor: "You put the killing thing right between your teeth, but you don't give it the power to do its killing."[2]

Gus enjoys playing combat video games and reading novelizations of them. Hazel tells Gus her favorite book is *An Imperial Affliction*, a novel narrated by Anna, a young girl with a rare blood cancer. Hazel has such strong feelings for the book she feels it is as much hers as her body and thoughts are hers. The book ends midsentence, and Hazel understands this means Anna has either died or gotten too sick to continue writing. Still, with the book lacking a proper conclusion, she is desperate to find out what happens to the other characters. She has written the author, Peter Van Houten, several letters, but he has never responded.

A Grand Gesture

Gus finds a way to e-mail Van Houten, and Hazel sends the author her questions. He replies he can only answer them in person, but he lives in the Netherlands. Soon after, Gus gives Hazel orange tulips, takes her to a huge sculpture called *Funky Bones* by a Dutch artist, and prepares a picnic with Dutch foods. After all these clues, he finally reveals he will use his wish from the Genies, an organization that grants special events to young people who are sick, to take Hazel to the Netherlands.

He touches her face and leans in to kiss her, but she tenses and pulls away. Later, she realizes why: she does not want to be a "grenade" and cause him pain when she dies.[3] She is aware Gus's former girlfriend died of cancer as well. Later, she texts him to say they can still be friends but she cannot kiss him.

The Netherlands

On the plane ride to the Netherlands, Gus tells Hazel he is in love with her, but she is too overcome to say anything back to him. The next day, they arrive at Van Houten's house, only to discover he is a rude eccentric with a drinking problem. He never intended for them

Gus and Hazel become even closer on their trip to Amsterdam.

to visit him in the Netherlands when he replied to their e-mail.

Hazel nevertheless persists with her questions about what happens to the characters in *An Imperial Affliction* after Anna's likely death. The author insults them and refuses to provide any answer other than to say the characters no longer exist once the novel ends. Hazel refuses to accept this reply. She smacks the drink out of Van Houten's hand, and she and Gus leave.

Van Houten's assistant, Lidewij, resigns on the spot. She takes Hazel and Gus to the Anne Frank House museum, where Hazel struggles with two steep flights of stairs. Hazel is deeply moved by the memory of Anne

Frank, a young woman who died in the Holocaust but left behind a diary filled with her inner thoughts about life. Lost together in the moment, Hazel and Gus kiss and are met with applause and cheers from the adults looking on.

Afterward, Hazel and Gus go to Gus's hotel room. Hazel finally tells Gus she loves him, and they lose their virginity to each other. The very next day, however, their love is put to the test. Gus tells Hazel he had a PET scan a few weeks earlier, and it showed his body is full of cancer. They both understand he will soon die.

Life without Gus

After returning home, Gus's condition quickly worsens and he is confined to a wheelchair. Hazel visits him almost every day. One day, Gus asks Hazel to prepare a eulogy and meet him at the church where they attend support group. When Hazel arrives, Gus reveals he has decided to hold a prefuneral. Only Hazel and their friend Isaac are there. In her eulogy, Hazel thanks Gus for giving her "a forever within the numbered days."[4]

Eight days later, Gus dies. Hazel delivers a different eulogy—one filled with platitudes to comfort the living—at his funeral. Van Houten attends the funeral, to Hazel's surprise. A few days later, Hazel is again surprised, this time finding Van Houten sleeping in the back of her parents' car. She learns he lost his eight-year-old daughter to cancer years ago and that writing about Anna in *An Imperial Affliction* was a way to give his daughter the teenage life she never had.

Shortly after the funeral, Isaac mentions to Hazel that Gus had been writing a sequel to *An Imperial Affliction* for her. Hazel searches Gus's house but cannot find it. Eventually, Hazel concludes Gus must have sent the piece to Van Houten. She contacts Lidewij, who manages to find the papers, but they instead turn out to be notes for Hazel's eulogy. Gus had wanted Van Houten to use the notes to write a proper eulogy, but Van Houten respectfully left the piece as is, admitting there was nothing more to add to it.

In the eulogy Hazel reads at the end of the novel, Gus says Hazel was truly heroic because she tried not to hurt people. He adds, "you don't get to choose if you get hurt in this world . . . but you do have some say in who hurts you. I like my choices. I hope she likes hers."[5] The novel ends with Hazel's response: "I do, Augustus. I do."[6]

Hazel never imagined Gus would die first.

9

Coming of Age amidst Tragedy

*I*n literature, a tragedy is a specific type of story that poses questions about the nature of human existence and suffering. In most cases, the protagonist of a tragedy comes to an unhappy or painful end—often death. This unhappy ending may be brought about by a hamartia, or fatal flaw, in the tragic hero, or main character. Typical hamartias include pride, greed, or ambition. In other tragedies, the tragic ending is brought about not by a hamartia but by fate. The tragedy genre dates back to ancient Greece, including dramas by Aeschylus and Sophocles. Playwright William Shakespeare is also well-known for tragedies, including *Romeo and Juliet*.

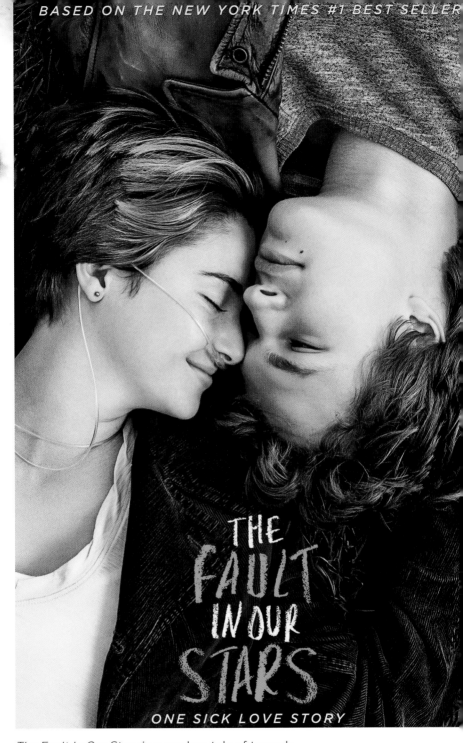

THE FAULT IN OUR STARS

ONE SICK LOVE STORY

The Fault in Our Stars is a modern tale of tragedy.

Hazel Grace Lancaster, the protagonist of John Green's *The Fault in Our Stars*, is a teenager living with terminal cancer. After meeting Augustus Waters, a cancer survivor and combat video game enthusiast, Hazel begins to see herself as a "grenade."[1] With the impending tragedy of her death, she fears she can only hurt her loved ones, like a grenade exploding in their hearts. Through her relationship with Gus, Hazel comes of age as she understands the true nature of tragedy—that one cannot love without pain.

Before meeting Gus, Hazel tries to minimize the emotional trauma her approaching death will cause the people she loves. Unable to attend high school, she is now distant from her once-close friends. She says they "wanted to help me through my cancer, but they

Thesis

The introduction ends with the thesis: "Through her relationship with Gus, Hazel comes of age as she understands the true nature of tragedy—that one cannot love without pain." The rest of the analysis will attempt to prove this statement.

Argument One

The first argument reflects how Hazel tries to protect her loved ones before she even begins her relationship with Gus: "Before meeting Gus, Hazel tries to minimize the emotional trauma her approaching death will cause the people she loves."

eventually found out that they couldn't. For one thing, there was no *through*."[2] Hazel is especially concerned about the impact her death will have on her parents, whom she considers her best friends. She believes the only thing worse than "biting it from cancer when you're sixteen" is "having a kid who bites it from cancer."[3] She is well aware she is the "alpha and omega of my parents' suffering," and she worries about their future.[4] That worry manifests in her obsession over the ending of *An Imperial Affliction*. She needs to know that even though Anna died, life went on for her parents as well as for the other characters.

As Hazel's relationship with Gus progresses, she begins to define herself with the grenade metaphor. She knows she has true feelings for Gus, but she tenses and resists when he tries to kiss her. Hazel's friend tells her perhaps it was due to a "premonition that there is something fundamentally incompatible and you're preempting the preemption."[5] Using video game imagery, Hazel takes the idea further,

Argument Two

The second argument focuses on how Hazel's dynamic with Gus shapes her grenade concept: "As Hazel's relationship with Gus progresses, she begins to define herself with the grenade metaphor."

imagining herself as a grenade: "I'm a grenade and at some point I'm going to blow up and I would like to minimize the casualties."[6] She fears deepening her relationship with Gus would be "committing an act of violence against him" because she will soon die.[7] She especially wants to protect him because he is drawn to grand gestures of sacrifice—whether it be jumping on grenades in video games or supporting a former girlfriend who died of cancer. Eventually, Hazel expresses her true feelings for Gus in Amsterdam. She accepts that he loves her, even if her impending death will hurt him: "I didn't want to be a grenade. But then again, he knew what he was doing. . . . It was his choice, too."[8]

But when she learns Gus will die first, Hazel fully understands what it means to be a grenade, and in doing so, she comes of age. Despite Hazel's fears of hurting Gus with her own death, it is actually he who will be the grenade to her. Wishing to spare her pain, he waits until after

Argument Three

The third argument shows Hazel's changing views as she moves into adulthood: "But when she learns Gus will die first, Hazel fully understands what it means to be a grenade, and in doing so, she comes of age."

94

Hazel realizes she cannot stand in the way of love—even if she is like a grenade.

their romantic day in Amsterdam to tell her he is dying. When he does share the news, he jokes he "had a hamartia after all."[9] His hamartia is not a fatal flaw of his own but—as the title suggests—a fault in his stars. That is, it is simply his fate to die of cancer first, even though they assumed he would outlive Hazel. Immediately, Hazel understands what it means to love someone amidst a tragedy: "Only now that I loved a grenade did I understand the foolishness of trying to save others from my own impending fragmentation."[10] She fully embraces love, even though she knows it will end in pain. Hazel's experience in loving and losing Gus also allows her to face her lingering fears about her parents' future. As her mother states, "You of all people know it is possible to live with pain."[11] With her deeper

As she comes of age, Hazel understands that love is full of tragedy.

understanding that love and pain are inseparable, Hazel steps into adulthood—even though she will likely not live much longer.

Similar to most tragedies, *The Fault in Our Stars* ends with death—Gus's death as well as Hazel's approaching death. But it also ends on a hopeful note about love, life, and the inevitable "grenades." As Gus writes to author Peter Van Houten, "You don't get to choose if you get hurt in this world . . . but you do have some say in who hurts you."[12] To experience love is to ultimately experience pain. Hazel knows she and Gus cannot conquer death, but she has found deeper meaning in love and life despite it. And that, the novel seems to say, is the true definition of tragedy.

Conclusion

The author wraps up the arguments and ties them back to the original thesis.

Thinking Critically

Now it is your turn to assess the essay. Consider these questions:

1. The critique is centered on Hazel's coming of age in the context of the grenade metaphor. Do any other metaphors affect her coming of age?

2. The author argues Hazel's obsession with *An Imperial Affliction* stems from her worry about her parents. What else could the book symbolize?

3. Do you agree with the author's claim that the book ends on a hopeful note?

Other Approaches

What you have just read is one possible way to analyze the tragic elements of *The Fault in Our Stars*. What are some other ways of applying this approach? Remember, a tragedy has to do with a character's downfall and the nature of suffering.

Aristotelian Approach

According to the Greek philosopher Aristotle, a tragedy should bring about catharsis in the audience. By this, he meant that audience members should feel pity and fear for the tragic hero so they are emotionally purified and uplifted. A thesis reflecting Aristotle's view of tragedy might be: As they deal with both the emotional and physical pain of living with cancer, Hazel and Gus bring catharsis for young readers who may or may not have direct experience with the disease.

Star-Crossed Lovers

Romeo and Juliet is often thought of as the epitome of star-crossed-lover tragedies. *The Fault in Our Stars* fits into this same genre. A thesis comparing the two works might be: Although *Romeo and Juliet* and *The Fault in Our Stars* both feature young lovers doomed by fate and circumstance, their endings leave readers with different conclusions about the nature of love and suffering.

Analyze It!

Now that you have examined the theme of coming of age, are you ready to perform your own analysis? You have read that this type of evaluation can help you look at literature in a new way and make you pay attention to certain issues you may not have otherwise recognized. So, why not look for a coming of age theme in one or more of your favorite books?

First, choose the work you want to analyze. How does the main character come of age? Are there secondary characters who also change or grow up? What external or internal factors affect how the characters change? If you choose to compare the theme in more than one work, what do they have in common? How do they differ? Next, write a specific question about the theme that interests you. Then you can form your thesis, which should provide the answer to that question. Your thesis is the most important part of your analysis and offers an argument about the work, considering the theme, its effect on the characters, or what it says about society or the world. Recall that the thesis statement typically appears at the very end of the introductory paragraph of your essay. It is usually only one sentence long.

After you have written your thesis, find evidence to back it up. Good places to start are in the work itself or in journals or articles that discuss what other people have said about it. You may also want to read about the author or creator's life so you can get a sense of what factors may have affected the creative process. This can be especially useful if you are considering how the theme connects to history or the author's intent.

You should also explore parts of the book that seem to disprove your thesis and create an argument against them. As you do this, you might want to address what others have written about the book. Their quotes may help support your claim.

Before you start analyzing a work, think about the different arguments made in this book. Reflect on how evidence supporting the thesis was presented. Did you find that some of the techniques used to back up the arguments were more convincing than others? Try these methods as you prove your thesis in your own critique.

When you are finished writing your critique, read it over carefully. Is your thesis statement understandable? Do the supporting arguments flow logically, with the topic of each paragraph clearly stated? Can you add any information that would present your readers with a stronger argument in favor of your thesis? Were you able to use quotes from the book, as well as from other critics, to enhance your ideas? Did you see the work in a new light?

Glossary

conscious
The part of the mind that a person is aware of at all times.

context
The words or statements that surround a word or idea in spoken or written communication and help to determine its meaning.

derogatory
Expressing a low opinion of someone or something; showing a lack of respect for someone or something.

displacement
The process of transferring one's feelings from a dangerous object to a safe one.

eulogy
A speech in honor of a person who has died, usually given at a funeral.

euthanasia
The practice of purposely ending the life of a person who is suffering.

immoral
Behavior that goes against accepted views of right and wrong.

irony
A method of using words to express the opposite of their literal meaning; dramatic irony is the contrast between what a character thinks to be true and what the audience knows.

literal
Based on the dictionary definition of a word; not figurative or symbolic.

metaphor
A figure of speech that compares two objects or ideas.

platitude
A dull or stale cliché.

reaction formation
A pattern of reversing the truth.

regression
A return to an earlier stage of development.

terminal
Fatal, ending in death.

unconscious
The part of the mind that holds thoughts, memories, and desires a person is unaware of but that influence behavior and emotions.

Characteristics
AND CLASSICS

Coming of age is a common theme in literature. A coming of age story typically features a teenage protagonist who matures into adulthood.

In this theme, the protagonist often does the following:

- Leaves childhood behind
- Gains wisdom and a new sense of identity
- Experiences a loss of innocence
- Understands society in a deeper way

Some famous works with a coming of age theme are:

- Charles Dickens's *Great Expectations*
- Louisa May Alcott's *Little Women*
- Betty Smith's *A Tree Grows in Brooklyn*
- Harper Lee's *To Kill a Mockingbird*
- J. K. Rowling's Harry Potter Series
- Khaled Hosseini's *The Kite Runner*

References

Baxter, Kent, ed. *Coming of Age*. Ipswich, MA: Salem, 2013. Print.

Green, John. *The Fault in Our Stars*. New York: Dutton, 2012. Print.

Green, John. "Questions about The Fault in Our Stars." *John Green*. n.d. Web. 24 Mar. 2015.

Knowles, John. *A Separate Peace*. 1959. New York: Scribner, 2003.

Lowry, Lois. *The Giver*. 1993. Boston: Houghton Mifflin, 2000. Kindle Fire.

Lynn, Steven. *Texts and Contexts: Writing About Literature with Critical Theory*. New York: Longman, 1998. Print.

McClinton-Temple, Jennifer. *Encyclopedia of Themes in Literature*. Vols. 1–3. New York: Facts on File, 2011. Print.

The Perks of Being a Wallflower. Dir. Stephen Chbosky. Summit Entertainment, 2012. DVD.

Salinger, J. D. *The Catcher in the Rye*. 1951. New York: Little, Brown, 2001. Print.

Spencer, Margaret Meek, and Victor Watson. *Coming of Age in Children's Literature*. New York: Continuum, 2003. Print.

Twain, Mark. *The Adventures of Huckleberry Finn*. 1885. Waxkeep, 2013. Kindle Fire.

Additional
RESOURCES

Further Readings

Graham, Sarah. *J.D. Salinger's* The Catcher in the Rye. New York: Routledge, 2007. Print.

Kupier, Kathleen, ed. *Prose: Literary Terms and Concepts*. New York: Britannica Educational/Rosen, 2012. Print.

Tolchin, Karen. *Part Blood, Part Ketchup: Coming of Age in American Literature and Film*. Lanham, MD: Lexington, 2007. Print.

Websites

To learn more about Essential Literary Themes, visit **booklinks.abdopublishing.com**. These links are routinely monitored and updated to provide the most current information available.

Places to Visit

Central Park Conservancy
14 East Sixtieth Street
New York, NY 10022
212-310-6600
http://www.centralparknyc.org
After leaving school, Holden Caulfield visits Central Park. Other locations Holden visits in New York City include the Museum of Natural History, Grand Central Station, and Radio City Music Hall.

Indianapolis Museum of Art
4000 Michigan Road
Indianapolis, IN 46208
317-923-1331
http://www.imamuseum.org
Gus takes Hazel on a picnic to *Funky Bones*, a sculpture by Dutch artist Joep Van Lieshout, located at the Indianapolis Museum of Art. The museum also includes collections of ancient and contemporary art from around the world.

The Mark Twain Boyhood Home and Museum
120 North Main Street
Hannibal, MO 63401
573-221-9010
http://www.marktwainmuseum.org
A visit to the museum includes a tour of Twain's childhood home as well as the home of Tom Blankenship, the boy who inspired the character of Huckleberry Finn.

Source Notes

Chapter 1. Introduction to Themes in Literature
None.

Chapter 2. An Overview of *A Separate Peace*
1. John Knowles. *A Separate Peace*. 1959. New York: Scribner, 2003. Print. 145.
2. Ibid. 194.

Chapter 3. The Symbolism of Coming of Age
1. John Knowles. *A Separate Peace*. 1959. New York: Scribner, 2003. Print. 46.
2. Ibid. 16.
3. Ibid. 59.
4. Ibid. 59.
5. Ibid. 72.
6. Ibid. 137.
7. Ibid. 159.
8. Ibid. 165.
9. Ibid. 191.
10. Ibid. 203.

Chapter 4. An Overview of *The Catcher in the Rye* and *The Perks of Being a Wallflower*
1. J. D. Salinger. *The Catcher in the Rye*. 1951. New York: Little, Brown, 2001. Print. 19.
2. Ibid. 214.
3. Ibid. 224–225.
4. Ibid. 251.
5. *The Perks of Being a Wallflower*. Dir. Stephen Chbosky. Summit Entertainment, 2012. DVD.
6. Ibid.

Chapter 5. Psychology and Coming of Age
1. J. D. Salinger. *The Catcher in the Rye*. 1951. New York: Little, Brown, 2001. Print. 3.
2. Ibid. 118.
3. Ibid. 102.
4. Ibid. 224–225.
5. *The Perks of Being a Wallflower*. Dir. Stephen Chbosky. Summit Entertainment, 2012. DVD.
6. J. D. Salinger. *The Catcher in the Rye*. 1951. New York: Little, Brown, 2001. Print. 13.
7. Ibid. 6–7.
8. *The Perks of Being a Wallflower*. Dir. Stephen Chbosky. Summit Entertainment, 2012. DVD.
9. J. D. Salinger. *The Catcher in the Rye*. 1951. New York: Little, Brown, 2001. Print. 67.
10. *The Perks of Being a Wallflower*. Dir. Stephen Chbosky. Summit Entertainment, 2012. DVD.
11. Ibid.
12. J. D. Salinger. *The Catcher in the Rye*. 1951. New York: Little, Brown, 2001. Print. 273–74.
13. *The Perks of Being a Wallflower*. Dir. Stephen Chbosky. Summit Entertainment, 2012. DVD.
14. Ibid.

Chapter 6. An Overview of *The Adventures of Huckleberry Finn* and *The Giver*

1. Mark Twain. *The Adventures of Huckleberry Finn*. 1885. Waxkeep, 2013. Kindle Fire.
2. Ibid.
3. Ibid.
4. Lois Lowry. *The Giver*. 1993. Boston: Houghton Mifflin, 2000. Kindle Fire.
5. Ibid.
6. Ibid.

Chapter 7. A Moralist View of Coming of Age

1. Mark Twain. *The Adventures of Huckleberry Finn*. 1885. Waxkeep, 2013. Kindle Fire.
2. Lois Lowry. *The Giver*. 1993. Boston: Houghton Mifflin, 2000. Kindle Fire.
3. Mark Twain. *The Adventures of Huckleberry Finn*. 1885. Waxkeep, 2013. Kindle Fire.
4. Ibid.
5. Ibid.
6. Lois Lowry. *The Giver*. 1993. Boston: Houghton Mifflin, 2000. Kindle Fire.
7. Ibid.
8. Mark Twain. *The Adventures of Huckleberry Finn*. 1885. Waxkeep, 2013. Kindle Fire.
9. Ibid.
10. Lois Lowry. *The Giver*. 1993. Boston: Houghton Mifflin, 2000. Kindle Fire.
11. Ibid.
12. Mark Twain. *The Adventures of Huckleberry Finn*. 1885. Waxkeep, 2013. Kindle Fire.
13. Ibid.

Chapter 8. An Overview of *The Fault in Our Stars*

1. John Green. *The Fault in Our Stars*. New York: Dutton, 2012. Print. 5.
2. Ibid. 20.
3. Ibid. 99.
4. Ibid. 260.
5. Ibid. 313.
6. Ibid. 313.

Chapter 9. Coming of Age amidst Tragedy

1. John Green. *The Fault in Our Stars*. New York: Dutton, 2012. Print. 89.
2. Ibid. 45.
3. Ibid. 7.
4. Ibid. 116.
5. Ibid. 95.
6. Ibid. 99.
7. Ibid. 101.
8. Ibid. 164.
9. Ibid. 215.
10. Ibid. 214.
11. Ibid. 295.
12. Ibid. 313.

Index

About the Author

Valerie Bodden has written more than 200 nonfiction books for children. Her books have received positive reviews from *School Library Journal*, *Booklist*, *Children's Literature*, *ForeWord Magazine*, *Horn Book Guide*, *VOYA*, and *Library Media Connection*. Valerie lives in Wisconsin with her husband and four young children. Visit her online at http://www.valeriebodden.com.